along the Navasota

AUTHOR & POET

SANDY CARROLL

Along the Navasota

Copyright © 2024 by **Sandy Carroll**

Published by tsk publishing © 2024
an imprint of Ohalla Productions
Corsicana, TX 75110   www.tskpublishing.com

Book & Cover Design © 2024 Local Talent
Artwork & BrushSources © 2024 - Andrewe, NightingaleCraftery, CraftyArter, Julia Dreams, Pickoloh, AlonaMAs, MikiBith, MiniMaxi, Uking, Separisa, Top Images, Anitapol, DADA, nataliahubbert, Veris Studio, LisaGlanz, NathanBrown, BrendaBakker, & LocalTalent

Along the Navasota/ Sandy Carroll

ISBN: 978-1-953348-42-5
Library of Congress Control Number: 2024914745

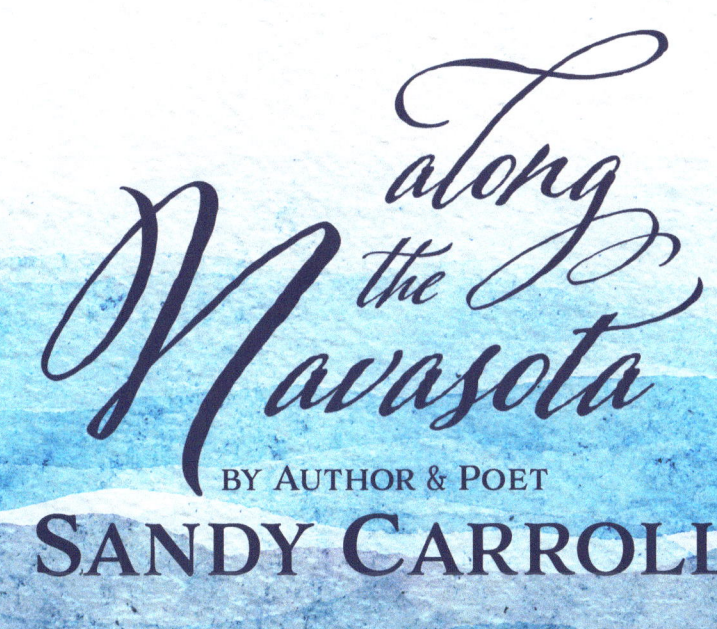

along the Navasota

BY AUTHOR & POET

SANDY CARROLL

**SOMETIMES THE DEEPER THE WATER,
THE HARDER WE HAVE TO SWIM.**

Along the Navasota is dedicated to
my brother Ronnie Carroll
and my son John Aulds.
They make it real.
~Sandy

CONTENTS

My Song of the Navasota

Memories instilled within concrete and steel,
  rekindle old flames in my heart,

Recapturing my soul, I'm captive once more,
  mesmerized by your seasonal art.

Today, you are still, as though remembering,
  like me, before age slips us into the past,

Laughter, excitement, contentment abound
  in woodsmoke's mysterious grasp.

Old Bridge, you're my youth, innocence lost,
  a friend that beckons my stay,

Where I sorted out life with its intense changes,
  deep where cottonwoods sway.

When my life's final chapter has come to end,
  may my ashes be tossed here by choice,

Where a barefoot child, with cane pole and dreams,
  in your arms will forever rejoice.

Sand Bass & Blackeyed Peas

Come back in time to a place with me,
  Where sand bass run and deer roam free.
With an old tackle box of homemade lures,
  And "You clean my fish and I'll cook yours!"

It's the quiet conversation on a hot afternoon,
  That echoes a river that winds to the moon.
Ride with me in a '49 Ford
  With a bushel of peaches on the running board,

To a family reunion by the riverside,
  Where chiggers were happy and new grandmothers cried.
And way down the river that familiar yell,
  "I caught one daddy! Bring the water pail!"

Then later that night, as they ate your fish,
  Everyone said it was the very best dish.
As evening fell and each lantern was lit,
  Trotlines were baited to the old folk's wit.

Then as the radio blared some Glen Miller tune,
  We danced barefoot 'neath an August moon.
And the world seemed right, folks were easy to please,
  In those days of sand bass and black-eyed peas.

By Lantern Light

On a winter night when the Milky Way casts its magic spell,
a skillet full of papermouths, will enhance one's sense of smell.
We used to place about fifteen poles with stoppers in a row,
then by lantern light we'd huddle, near the river's chilly flow.
When a cork would bounce, then disappear, the closest kid would run
to grab that pole and get the perch–it was loads of fun.
We'd make our camp by a large brush pile where the river ran so deep,
keeping those perch hooks baited up, kept us on our feet.
One night, a cold blue norther hit, and the crappie went to bitin',
so many stoppers went out of sight, the kids all got to fightin'.
We landed fifty or sixty fish in about three hours' time,
then drank coffee by the cupful as dawn touched timberline.
Sleepy-eyed, we'd head for home, fishin' stories in our head,
of those big white perch on a hunger binge, where sunset lingers red.

The Boots

Over by that stump rests a pair of boots
   if only they could speak

'Bout stumbling through both briar and mud
   campfire ash and creek

They've hunted deer, wild hogs, and quail
   where most folks fear to trod

And listened to a whippoorwill
   while their owner talked to God

      These boots know fear of lightning
        and have felt a rattler's bite

          They've rested by a pot of beans
            as day turned into night

            This is why I'll keep these boots
              there's stories in the leather

            'Bout living to the fullest
              as life's seasons blend together

Maggie

Sticker bushes, hollers, creek beds, and swamps,
   my Bluetick always eager to run
A snake-killing, fish-biting, coon-treeing canine
   always ready for the lowering sun
Baying like an opera singer with her girdle too tight
   even a deaf coon could hear
That thrashing and crunching through dead fall and vine
   alerted them Maggie was near
Halfway up the tree, she would glance back at me
   desperate to bring her prize down
Slowly I aimed, enjoying the rush
   and brought that coon to the ground
How many sunrises we greeted
   covered in a blanket of fog
Just Maggie and me sharing biscuits,
   side by side on some rotten log

The Tacklin' Conversation

While on vacation the other day,
   I stopped at Sam's Tackle Store,
Enjoying the cool, I was amazed to see
   what folks were asking for!

Some were grabbing Wiggle Warts, Rat-L-
   Traps, and Crazy Shad,
One lady brought a Floating Frog,
   she claimed would make fish mad!

Two fishin' guides were loading up
   with packs of red/flaked worms,
Lake Fork their destination,
   to bring some hawgs to sudden terms.

Munching on granola bars,
   I overheard two elderly men,
Talking about the early days
   when they fished Toledo Bend.

"If they had made them gold-flaked
   worms when I was in my prime,
Every record for Texas bass
   definitely would be mine!"

A young father with his six-year-old,
   buying minnows by the door,
Exclaimed, "This will be a panfish day,
   we've got lot of fun in store!"

Aggies headed for Gibbons Creek
   had bought a brand new net,
Asked about maroon and white worms,
   but they hadn't been invented yet!

Up on the counter were black Jitterbugs
   for three anglers to use that night,
They said that on a midnight run,
   these lures would work just right.

About the time I found a chair,
   a women's club came in,
Now the action in that tackle shop
   was truly to begin!

"We want Mustad Hooks, Stanley jigs,
 spinnerbaits, and spoons,
Plastic worms, surface plugs,
 –excuse us, we need some room!

Do you carry those new CrazyTails
 that dart, dance, and dive,
And some Acme Little Cleo lures
 that make' um come alive?

Also we need some gasoline,
 and check those trailer wheels,
We're using my husband's Ranger boat,
 and also his rod and reels!"

Through the glass front door,
 Sam and I watched them load their gear,
"Did you know that lady driving that rig
 won $85,000 last year?"

My mouth fell open in total surprise,
 "You mean she was a pro?"
"One of the best, and she's taking her
 friends where the big 'uns grow!"

My watch said ten, it was time to leave,
 but I had learned a lot,
The problem was, in all this confusion,
 my list–I had forgot!

So standing in the center aisle,
 I let out a desperate sigh,
"Would someone in this tackle store
 please tell me what to buy?"

Blue Norther

Grayish-Blue clouds rolled in from the north,
   Whitecaps flipped spray in the air,
A Texas blue norther was picking up force,
   I was just glad we were there!
Most trophy-sized bass had been caught in the cold,
   The temp was now dropping real fast,
With my grape-colored worms, and a thermos of java,
   I definitely intended to last!
My partner was casting with a jig-and-eel bait,
   His cheeks turning red from the cold,
He was mumbling some statement that if we didn't leave soon,
   We would lose our last chance to grow old!
Cold air was whistling up the legs of my jeans,
   When I felt a sharp tap on my line,
Just as I'd hoped, a pre-spawning bass!
   This cold snap was just short of divine.
Froze, but excited, my friend grabbed the net,
   As I brought that nine-pounder around,
After bringing her in, we headed for camp,
   To show off this lunker we'd found!
Later that night by a warm, roaring fire,
   We savored the memory of that big fish,
Blue Norther had passed, history was made,
   For this angler had gotten his wish.

The River

The river drifts slowly with its permanent tears of fishermen long ago
Uninterrupted, I cast, breathless, anticipating some mystery below
Flashes of sun perch and dragonfly, silver shad escaping the deep
Hoping my lures on their journey will startle a prize from its sleep
Instilled in my youth, this vigil, to sportsmen I need not explain
We seek silent refuge in habitats of whitetail, black bass, and crane
God dwells in places of quietude where beauty is hard to define
The only time stillness is broken is the snap of my old fishing line
When shadows turn purple before dark descends,
I'll remember this respite today
Leave a few tears in the river, then reluctantly go on my way

The Returning

In a slant of light on the forest floor, dove season opened its gate
Sitting on knees of a walnut tree, I could hardly wait
My grandpa and my father hunted here before
A handed-down old rifle, how could I ask for more
Whip like fronds of a willow celebrated this returning,
Woodsmoke draped the creek bed from my camp stove slowly burning
Unexpected experiences like a Norther's sudden chill
Raccoons enjoying remnants of my anticipated meal
First taste of wild hog meat beneath a bed of coals
Introduction to "no-see-ums" crawling up a knoll
Today, I donned a flannel shirt, history on its sleeves
Remembered following Daddy in a swirl of falling leaves

Memories

My very first rod, at the ripe age of nine,
  Was a piece of equipment I considered divine!
Nature my heart-throb, fishin' my love,
  That reel and I joined the bass and the dove.

My first ten-pound catfish nearly scared me to death,
  And a nine-pound black bass took all of my breath,
Are memories for me and this old rod and reel.
  To all those who fish, you know how I feel.

In the quiet of rivers with the sun at my back,
  I grew up with God, there was nothin' I lacked.
With my old, blue-tick hound named Slew on my heels,
  I roamed every foot of these wildflowers fields.

Mama would tell me, "Go catch me some fish!"
  Then me and old hound would grant her that wish.
Today I'm an angler with a nice fishin' rig,
  Equipped with spinners, buzz baits, and jigs.

But I find there are times when I again long to be,
  Just a kid on the river with a heart wild and free.
With a sack of cold biscuits in a shallow lagoon,
  Where crystal clear water is kissed by the moon.

The Family Fish

Scrambled eggs were cooking,
   and the coffee nearly perked,
When my little brother's
   long cane pole
   gave a sudden jerk.

Squealing like a baby pig,
   he picked it up to run,
That's when the battle of the
   family fish had suddenly begun.

I saw him lose his footing,
   then plunge into the stream,
Into the air I threw my rod,
   as he let out a scream.

My mother bending over
   to taste the food just cooked,
Cried out in pain and agony,
   snagged by my flying hook!

Holding on with all my might
   to my brother's curly locks,
I braced myself
   as the muddy water
   filled my shoes and socks.

Finally, Dad came around the bend
   upon this crazy sight,
Docked his boat and quickly came
   to help relieve our plight.

Pulling out my brother,
   then helping me get free,
He went to aid my mother,
   now bawling near a tree,

With pocket knife and patience,
   he removed my treble hook,
As mother gave each one of us
   a fierce and angry look!

Right below our fishin' spot,
   in a clump of tangled brush,
My baby brother's pole had lodged,
   and we bolted in a rush!

Still on the line
   was a nine-pound cat,
   his tail too tired to swish,
We dubbed our prize
   that day at lunch,
   our entire family's fish!

13

The Hunt

Velvety curtains of thunderheads brought forth a pitchfork rain,

the dripping tent flaps beckoned sleep to a weary hunter's brain.

All day hunts with no results, most would feel dismay.

But it's not the kill the heart desires, it's the healing time away.

It's the whir and blur of beating wings, a pillow's wood-smoked smell,

eager eyes with dampened paws, beside you on the trail.

It's the feel of a handed-down double-barrel

at port arms when daylight breaks,

coffee boiling the old-fashioned way alongside simmering steaks.

When my shadow in life starts lengthening,

to young hunters I surely will say,

It's not the kill the heart desires, but the healing time away.

Grandpa Takes Me Fishin'

Grandpa's always busy with his chores around the farm,
But he's the best pal that I have, when the weather turns off warm.
He'll dig some worms, catch those hoppers, then to the creek we go,
Then all day long we fish and talk and talk as summer breezes blow.
Grandpa doesn't mind at all the fact I cannot walk,
We may be slower getting there, but we have more time to talk.
I can bait my hook, cast out, and bring those bass on in,
But the nicest part of the entire day is being there with him!
He gave me on old fishin' hat with lures stuck in it's side,
There is no doubt that I must be the source of Grandpa's pride.
When I grow up and face this world's adventures on my own,
My goal is to be a gentle guy, like Grandpa, when I'm grown.
He never seems to notice this wheelchair that I'm in,
Thank you, Lord, for fishin' days, and Gramps, my dearest friend.

Trotline

When I turned eight, my dad decided
    to let me learn the river,
To paddle his boat, untangle the line,
    and slice the chicken liver.
So, all one summer on weekend nights,
    we ran his old trotline.
What I learned of nature and solitude
    is still hard to define!
So quiet we were with separate thoughts,
    but engulfed in God's domain,
As crickets chirped, bullfrogs croaked,
    anticipating rain.
While baiting up as the sun went down,
    we talked and laughed and dreamed,
But later when we ran our line,
    we were set for 'something mean!"

Dad would say, "A fifty-pounder could
    yank you from this boat!"
I'd pull the anchor across my lap,
    and fear would squeeze my throat.
I tried to keep the line real low
    until we'd reach our captured prize,
Then when I flipped it in the boat,
    pride shone within Dad's eyes.
How many times at two a.m.,
    we shared a cheese and cracker meal.
If you ever ran a trotline,
    then you know just how I feel.
Dad would clean our mess of fish,
    as he sang some funny tune,
As I learned about the river,
    underneath a trotline moon.

Gone Fishin'

Removing myself from life's mundane restraints,
    I left word that I had gone fishin'.
An afternoon's encounter with a Texas black bass,
    was a thrill for which I'd been wishin'.
Mist blanketed the river near some heavy moss beds,
    as the sun turned her face in a cloud.
Gone fishin' was the best way for a person in need,
    to escape from the maddening crowd!
I reached in my lure box for a Culprit ten-inch,
    which had caught many hawgs in the past.
Gone fishin' might result in a memory today,
    a personal experience to last.
Then my line twitched, I reared back on my rod,
    and attempted to drive that steel home!
I cranked through hydrilla which seemed to hold the bass,
    turning the water to foam!
In just a few moments the black bass was mine,
    tranquility again filled my soul.
Gone fishin' would continue to be the best medicine,
    for a middle-aged guy growing old.

19

The Showdown

Daylight found my coffee mug
   next to my tackle box,
      As spring began to lift her windless fog.

Silence met determination
   as I searched with mortal eye,
      For I sensed old bucketmouth around that log.

Every year we met right here,
   hydrilla was his game.
      We seemed to know each other's every thought.

He'd slash water in my boat,
   I had hooked him twice,
      But he pitched back every lure I ever bought!

Throw, retrieve, all morning long;
   I sometimes saw his wake,
      And I knew his strike, like lightning, would be soon.

My hands began to tremble
   as I glanced down at my watch,
      Two minutes and the time would be high noon!

Just like an old-time gunfighter,
   I reached slowly for a lure,
      A Bomber's Rip Shad just might bring him in.

Thirty seconds now to go,
   sweat wrinkled from my brow,
      Waiting for this battle to begin.

Busting from beneath his log,
   he grabbed the silver bait,
      Then leaping high, he shook with all his might!

Both feet braced, elbows locked,
   leaning slightly left,
      This showdown had now turned into a fight!

I set my hook it seemed three times,
   and never gave him slack,
      He walked green water right before my eyes,

Never seen a prettier sight
   in all my fishin' days,
      Black bass against a pale blue Texas sky!

Duck Hunter's Prayer

When the blood of Autumn's dying leaves
scatter around my feet,
And the mystical backwoods beckon me home,
my Master there to greet,
I'll remember the fabric of yesterday,
canvas, flannel and tweed,
The feel of my shotgun pressed to my chest,
crouching where ducks light to feed.
Saint Peter may tell me my coffee is bad
and to leave my wet boots at the gate,
I'll then hold up my limit and try to explain
that this is the reason I'm late.
If my Master will take me I'll make one request,
and duck hunters will know what I mean,
That my halo shine bright like a moonlit night,
and my wings be camouflage green.

The Camp

Tracing the moon's rising shadow
    from my sleeping bag close by the fire,
Solitude engulfed me like an old flannel coat,
    such a wonderful way to retire.
Gunny, my coon hound, lay watchful,
    alert to the sounds of the night.
I knew my old pal was thinking
    about Canada geese taking flight.
Close by my head lay grandpa's treasure,
    how I wished this prize shotgun could talk.
It was slung on his shoulder and carried,
    long before I was able to walk.
Somewhere in heaven I hope grandpa knows,
    the joy that he handed down,
These embers glow bright on this duck hunter's night,
    as my childhood memories abound.

Ghost Bass

A legend is whispered around tournament fires,
    about a guide who caught a ghost!
It's usually told around midnight,
    over scrambled eggs and toast.
I listened to this talk one night,
    and my skin began to crawl.
This incident supposedly happened last year,
    on Lake Fork in the fall.
This guide went out night bassin',
    and had caught and eight-pound hawg,
Then quietly dropped another lure,
    next to a rotten log.
The surface temp was seventy-two,
    a pale moon overhead,
When suddenly he sensed an unusual chill,
    his rod then turned to lead!
Up from the depths a monster bass,
    thirty pounds at least,
Slammed into his Skeeter boat
    for a bait-devouring feast!
Scrambling for his largest lure,
    the angler hurried fast,
Water churned from the grimy deep,
    as he made another pass!

Three Stanley jigs and a piece of pork
    he made into a lure,
Throwing it madly through the air,
    this mess would work for sure!
That monster bass took all three lures,
    and spit 'em in the boat!
Then the thirty pounds of bucket-mouth
    tried to grab him by his throat!
He started up his engine
    and tried to pull away,
But nobody's seen that fishin' guide,
    nor his boat, right up to this very day!
Some folks claim when the moon is full,
    that ghost black bass can be seen,
Thirty pounds of silver hell,
    and looking awful mean!
Just one piece of that Skeeter boat
    was found up in a tree.
I hadn't believed in ghosts before,
    but I won't disagree!
If you go night bassing and the air turns cold,
    and you spot a swirling mass,
You may be meeting near some ol' rotten log,
    Lake Fork's Ghostly Bass!

The Beginners

It was summer of 1959,
  but the memory lives today
my brother-in-law, Eddie the banker,
  needed to get away

The Navasota River,
  like a mirror splashed in green
was awakened by our tiny boat
  with its roar like a washing machine

Neither of us had caught a bass,
  and I'm sure the bass all knew
and after replacing four shear pins,
  we decided what to do

Just drift along, from log to log,
  on a breeze out of the south,
but that idea changed in haste,
  after a brush with a cottonmouth

Thirsty, hot, and hungry,
    but filled with want for bass,
we decided we would tough it out
    –surely we could last

It must have been around 5 o'clock
    when he overshot the bank,
then, cussin' about the underbrush,
    he slowly tried to crank

But his lure took off for parts unknown,
    the reel began to spin,
I sat straight up and braced myself
    for whatever he'd bring in

Then finally, after struggling hard,
    his trophy could be seen,
I laughed so hard the tears popped out
    and he just looked real mean

After removing the hook from the roadrunner's wing,
    which seemed to be OK,
he glanced at me and said real low,
    "Never mention what happened today"

The years have flown–he's a pro angler now,
    but I want the final word,
I've fished with a lot of different folks since then,
    but not one has landed a bird

Ictalurus Furcatus

My grandma was a fishin' fiend, in search of channel cat,
    Not only did she crave their taste,
        she knew where they were at!
    I'd help her on a winter morn, get all the things she'd need,
        Chicken livers, cornflakes and soap,
            and cakes of cottonseed.

She'd search for a green and mossy place, where a current swept the bank,
    Then we'd start setting those limb lines out,
        — the smell got pretty rank!
    "Be sure you wrap a good-size piece of stink bait around that hook,"
        I'd dig down in that bucket of mess,
            but I couldn't stand to look!

"I hope it rains this afternoon, if it does we've got it made!"
    All I wanted, amidst the spiders and heat,
        was a glass of lemonade.
    Finally finished, we headed home, Granny had the biggest smile,
        "Come midnight we'll have some fish!
            Aren't you excited child?"

She tended her chores, cleaned the house, and fixed a wondrous meal,
    Then she and Gramps talked on the porch
        as they gazed across their field.
    I drifted to sleep in the porch swing to the sound of distant thunder,
        And Grandma saying, "I'll bet right now
            every catfish limb's gone under!"

About eleven p.m., she woke me up with a flashlight in my face,
    I knew real soon I'd be invading
        Mr. Ictalurus Furcatus' place!
    From our boat, we lifted each line and every bait was gone,
        But watching Granny's eagerness,
            I was glad I'd come along,

Line number twelve held the jackpot fish that all our work was for!
    The limb was bent, the water swirled,
        it acted like a gar.
    "Don't get too close, he'll go berserk and straighten out that hook!"
        Then Grandma picked a huge gaff up,
            and took on a stubborn look.

She eased her hand around the line as I lowered our long-handled net,
    My knees were knocking, my breathing short,
        I couldn't see for sweat.
    Suddenly together we pulled him in, a monster we had found,
        By the time I got him in the net,
            I was nearly drowned.

Fifty pounds of channel cat pitched heavily in the boat,
    Granny laughed when I moved my feet,
        as fear clutched at my throat!
    I'll never forget that winter day with nature in perfect tune,
        Us dragging that cat, as coyotes howled
            by the light of a quarter moon.

On Butler's Pond

It was perch-jerkin' time on Butler's Pond,
    not even a chance of a breeze.
July's dog days had sent typical anglers
    scurrying for the shade of some tree.

My friend Johnny Hawk in the end of the boat,
    was casting and reeling away.
At one hundred degrees, it was too hot to talk,
    as we watched baby turtles play.

A teacher of math, he was figuring our chances
    of landing a record-sized bass.
When all of a sudden a monstrous swirl,
    something was making a pass!

All of the scrambling and talking we did,
    flinging those top-water plugs.
Old Mossback was definitely checking us out,
    while searching for low-flying bugs.

From that watery oven he rose bustin' air,
  no doubt he would go seven pounds.
Johnny nervously grabbed a black, floating worm,
  hoping he'd come back around.

Pitching his bait across thick vegetation,
  he then wiggled it back through the moss.
Suddenly the battle of the big bass began,
  soon we'd know who was the boss!

After several bold runs, the hawg hung in the weeds,
  and old Johnny retrieved him in style.
With a backdrop of willows, and blue sky overhead,
  we relished this moment a while.

As the sun hoisted shadows, we quietly observed,
  her features like ours had been changing.
How gradual it seemed here on Butler's Pond,
  as nature went about rearranging.

What keeps us traveling hundreds of miles?
  What enticement does this lair possess?
Simple illusions of a whippoorwill call,
  that fishin' right here is the best.

Mr. Alligator Gar

We had just settled down for an afternoon snooze,
   with our fishin' poles neatly set out.
That August sun was hot enough
   to broil a speckled trout.
My cousin's feet were dangling
   in the water near some moss,
Just inches away, Mr. Alligator Gar
   was looking for a frog he'd lost.
I guess the sight of those kicking feet
   meant game for Mr. Gar.
He zeroed in and grabbed some toes,
   and we ran for our car!
Out to the middle of the river he went,
   with my cousin pulling back,
"Hang on," I yelled, as I got my gun
   to stop that gar attack.
My shooting didn't do a thing
   but make old gar real mad.
By then my cousin was hugging a log,
   in a school of silver shad.
Then up from the depths came a snapping turtle,
   eighty pounds at least!

He gripped that gar with those big sharp jaws,
    he'd found himself a feast!
My cousin swam that river channel,
    two feet above the foam,
And never stopped to say goodbye,
    he was headed home.
It's been three years since that awful day
    when cousin lost his toe.
We still invite him fishin',
    but his answer's always, "No!"
The other day we saw a gar
    with scars across his side,
I now believe old snapper
    was the one that day who died.
The moral to this story is,
    you just can't kill a gar.
If one comes up, just pack your gear
    and head out for the car!

Over the Dam

One bright sunny day I was casting the bank
  beside the Fort Parker Dam,
When off in the distance two anglers appeared
  in a jon-boat totally jammed!

Drinking and laughing, they kept roaring ahead,
  making no effort to turn,
My arm waving gestures to warn them to stop
  were ignored as they steadily churned.

Twenty feet from the dam one guy stood up,
  now stunned at their oncoming plight,
Oars began flying, but it was too late,
  I have never seen such a sight!

I ran down the shoreline to the edge of the dam,
  in my heart I just knew they were dead!
But far down below, they were baiting their hooks,
  one fisherman scratching his head.

"Are you two okay?" I yelled out of breath,
  still mumbling my now answered prayer.
"Yeah, we're alright, but the main problem is,
  how do we get back up there?"

The Fishin' Dog

Down in East Texas
    where the swamp meets the river',
        there lives a fishin' dog!
To get a fish
    he'll swim the river,
        or even ride a hollow log.
He'll sit on the bank
    and point like a setter,
        'til your cork goes outta sight.
When you bring it in,
    he'll jump that fish,
        and fasten on real tight.
That hound won't rest
    'til he knows for sure
        that perch is on the stringer,
Then back to the edge,
    to whine at the pole,
        like a starving opera singer!
His master, an old,
    whiskered feller
        by the name of
        Moss McGee,
Said he found that dog
    when he was a pup
        in the top of a
            cypress tree.

There had been a flood
    the week before, and that pup
        had been there since.
He couldn't get down,
    so he learned to fish,
        just used some common sense.
Now this old dog
    can't bait a hook,
        and he's never learned to cast,
But he might be able
    to row a boat,
        I flat out forgot to ask.
I guess right now
    as the sun goes down
        in that thick, East Texas fog,
            Old man McGee
                is frying some perch
                    for him and
                        his fishin' dog.

35

SANDY CARROLL

The Hunting Shack

Sudden rain fallin' on a rusty tin roof,
    venison stew bubbling hot
Sleepy eyes gazing at cobwebs,
    draped above antler and cot
Damp socks stiffening on a pot-bellied stove,
    tales of hunts long ago
My wet dog's smell mixed with honing oil,
    slight possibility of snow
Deer graze the hollow, ducks feed in the marsh,
    tomorrow, we hunt for the prize
Excitement apparent, no sleep tonight
    in this shelter for coon dogs and guys
Wooden decoys and hand-carved lures
    reflected in the globe of a lamp
Most of them made before I was born
    back then, they called this "the camp"
Dominos clacking, wood turning to ash,
    quiet moon rising over the timber
When I get too old to make it up here,
    I'll have these good times to remember

The Duck Hunter

In a tangle of cattails with fuzz on his hat,
where waterfowl drop in for the night,
my grandfather's spirit must surely reside
catching the last rays of light.
He's paddling through marshes of mallard and teal,
hypnotized by their quiet nesting grounds.
Relishing the songs from feather and bone,
where total harmony resounds.
Did he teach me the flyways of seasonal change,
did he make me a duck hunter, too?
At this moment, I'm waiting for a winged silhouette
dropping gracefully from out of the blue.

Call of the Bass

The old man on the porch
   heard the call of the bass
      on the wind that whirled leaves 'cross his yard
Somewhere up the river,
   he knew they were waitin'
      for this seasonal change from the Lord
Mist would be forming
   like the tears in his eyes
      for no longer could he answer the call
But his memories were mounted
   with weights, dates, and places,
      all lining the living room wall
Down the street a young father
   helped his son load their gear
      He smiled as they hurried to leave
When the call of the bass
   touches the soul
      the adventures are hard to perceive
As the breeze grabbed the chill,
   he turned in for the night
      as peacefulness flooded his heart
There's a gift in just knowing
   the call of the bass
      A true fisherman knows from the start

Old Buck

The pulse of the river seemed in unison with mine,
  melancholy at the passing of day
An elusive old buck I'd been tracking,
  was by now, too far away
Tonight in a thicket, head up and alert,
  the buck would hardly take rest

Knowing tomorrow he'd be hunted again,
  his agility put to the test
What he doesn't know is I'm older now
  like him, I have changed quite a lot
It's cameras I carry instead of a gun
  for a photo instead of a shot
We're both seeking refuge
  for a peaceful old age
    among thicket, canebrake, and wood
I'd share a warm fire and
  commune with this deer,
    if there was some way that I could

The Tournament

They called him a clod-kickin' hayseed,
    in his wooden fishing boat.
Yet, he had his entry fee
    tucked in his faded coat.

When daylight came they roared away,
    left him in their wake.
Then he gave his grandad's Evinrude
    all that it could take.

Big rigs raced to the "weigh-in" all day,
    in hopes of an hourly prize.
He was content to cast under a bridge,
    competition in disguise.

Grandpa's favorite lure took flight,
    then the shallows churned.
Upon its tail, the huge bass danced,
    a trick old moss had learned.

The deadline came, he made it,
   with his twelve-pound flopping bass.
Not a word was said from a startled crowd,
   they grinned and let him pass.

In a wheelchair by a worn-out truck,
   an old man's hand was shaking.
"That's my grandson over there,"
   his voice had started breaking,

"I taught him it's not what you have,
   determination is the key.
Excuse me, folks, I think he wants
   his picture made with me."

Angler's Prayer

I thank Thee, Lord, for these hands of mine
that can lift a rod and reel
For the solitude on the riverbank
as I fix myself a meal
Thank You for each starry night
that I have pitched a tent
Where catfish ran, a full moon rose
for all these times You've sent
I thank Thee, Father, for these eyes of mine
that've caught a sunset's gold
These memories I will treasure
when I take to growing old
You've protected me when the tide was high
and the strong winds began to rise
And guided my rig to a harbor safe
beneath dark, violent skies
You've taught me, God,
through the great outdoors
to see that life is fair
So I thank Thee, Father,
on bended knee
as I send this 'Angler's Prayer'

Ode to the Hunter

Deep in the soul of those drawn to hunt
  is a place never-changing its pace
Where solitude dwells in the tracks of a deer
  and quiet wears a spiritual face

Cares of the day seem to bounce off the wind
  over the front of an old pick-up grill
Then, by evening, a campfire and a skillet of stew
  finds the spirit renewed in its will

Somewhere in the pages of a hunter's log
  there are traces of an artist at work
Describing the sunrise, the sunset, and the moon
  while awaiting the coffee to perk

There's an old lantern burning in a sportsman's dreams
  reflecting the end of the day
When a limit of ducks and the company of friends
  keep all of life's troubles away

No Conversation Needed

Like a still-life composition,
   he sits there on the pier
Tweed and leather jacket zipped,
   a Norther drawing near

Autumn sunlight fading fast
   as he casts into the wind
No conversation needed
   from this sportsman, dad, and friend

He has shown me mallards in the fog,
   taught me campfire songs
Tied my lures, packed my gear,
   taught me right from wrong

We've hunted turkey, deer, and quail;
   fished river, lake, and creek
Through the solitude of wilderness,
   somehow our souls could speak

His hair now white, mine turning grey,
   like seasons ages blend
No conversation needed
   from this sportsman, dad, and friend

The Blessing

One Last Hunt in pursuit of a Buck
Alone and one hundred years old.
The old Veteran knew it would be his last,
As he walked through the mist in the cold.
Then in a clearing, his Blessing appeared,
History repeated itself.
Both realized in an instant
They were the only ones left.
The essence of Nature surrounded the scene,
As the old man sat in the leaves.
One last glance at Winter
Settling itself in the trees.
I miss his smile and stories,
As I sip from his coffee cup
And retrace his steps to the clearing,
Knowing he never gave up.

45

Saltwater Battle

In pouring down rain, my brother and I,
  were shoulder to shoulder that day.
With sixty more anglers on a hundred-foot pier,
  tasting the salt and the spray.
All baited up with those large, silver shad,
  that cost two dollars a piece!
Our reward, though, would be later that day,
  when we tossed redfish in some grease.
Two hours had passed with rain in our faces,
  when Ronnie's big reel did a spin!
"Pull out your lines!" I yelled to the folks,
  "So my brother can bring him on in!"
Thirty minutes he battled, his arms growing tired,
  teeth clenched, eyes straight ahead.

Why couldn't he surface this monstrous fish?
    his face now turning red!
Then over behind him on the side of the pier,
    I noticed a strange, shocking sight.
Another tough angler was identically matching,
    my own brother's exhausting plight.
As one bent and reeled, the other one rose,
    they were hooked to each other's test line.
When I yelled out this fact, what each gentleman said,
    I'm not at liberty now to define!
With everyone laughing they grinned and shook hands,
    like two good sporting fishermen should.
Then under his breath, my brother declared,
    "I'd shove that guy off this pier, if I could!"

A Honey Hole Summer

The breeze had been trapped by a curtain of pine,
Puffy clouds, as though tamed, seemed standing in line.
A shutter-eyed lizard, stretched in lime-colored light,
Watched some shad swimming quietly, unaware of their plight.
Near some thick submerged timber, Old Mossback was waiting,
For the silver-streaked dinner he had been anticipating.
I had been taught by my dad to have a "big bass attitude."
So, I picked a large spinner as his probable food.
I threw my first cast near a small school of shad,
And the second it hit, they whirled, suddenly glad.
For out from the timber wet fury lunged past,
Almost yanking the rod from my now trembling grasp.
Emerald green water turned a foaming white blur,
It seemed creatures nearby knew what fate would occur.
This old lunker'd been dominating this hole for a while,
Now losing is freedom, he was going in style.
Below, how he twisted, the lure set through his lip,
He tried all his known tactics to give me the slip.
Some sunfish and crawfish by a large lily pad,
Were relieved by his capture, as were the small shad.
As nature rebalanced in her strange, wondrous way,
Old Mossback had provided me "a honey hole day."

Made in America

Some companies who design hunting clothes
   never endured a Texas Norther.
Ferocious, whipping, icy wind
   that will bend those shoulders forward.
It enters those layers of high-dollar gear,
   reaches places you can't get to.
Some areas inside my hip waders,
   I feel is turning blue.
I don't remember Grandpa and Dad
   dressing like this when they left the farm.
Hunted all day in flannel and wool,
   then came home, their feet were still warm.
"Made in America" makes the difference
   when hunting in the wild.
I still use things they handed down
   when I was just a child.
They didn't get breakfast in the drive-thru,
   it came off the stove at home.
Thick white gravy, cathead biscuits,
   ham, right off the bone.
I miss them, and I miss "American Made"
   as I wade across the stream,
feeling the water seeping in
   from the rips in my Neoprene.

Shovel Bum

I was a Shovel Bum, diggin' fishing worms,
   the wind was from the West.
White Perch tugging at my heart-lines
   wearing Grandpa's vest.
Watching bobbers invited long chats,
   as we swatted mosquitos and buffalo gnats.
Gramps likes a Pearl beer and a bowl of Red
   off his tailgate by the riverbed.
"Don't yank the cork," would echo,
   I was a headstrong kid, you know.
Bare feet dangling in the water,
   at spooky things below.
He watched me like a chicken hawk
   because I had no sense of fear.
My Guardian Angel of the great outdoors,
   he was my Papa dear.
When sundown bends his Coleman's glow
   outside my canvas tent,
I gaze into the starry night
   'cause that's where I know he went.

Nowadays

Accepting the fact my fishin' nowadays
    is reliving old memories I've made.
Passersby aren't aware that I'm tossin' out lures
    from this rocking chair here in the shade.
When I'm dozing lightly, and they think I'm asleep,
    I'm cleaning a stringer of bass.
Just feeling the warmth of a campfire
    as a couple of loons make a pass.
I find my comfort in familiar old friends
    tacklebox, shotgun, and reel.
As long as they're close by, I'm happy.
    Any sportsman knows how I feel.
Nowadays my energy is sporadic,
    sporting naps I take during the day.
But beneath surface dreams, fish are biting,
    as fall willows tremble and sway.
Never worry when I gaze out my window
    for what seems like hours on end.
In thoughts, I'm unrolling the old sleeping bag,
    as a flight of mallards descend.

Choices

Between wing and river in shadowy mist
    where tree roots twisted to drink
Embracing the quiet, mysterious morn
    watching the sunrise of pink
Velvety antlers, huge cautious eyes
    suddenly appeared from the bush
I picked up my rifle, adjusted my scope,
    enjoying the adrenaline rush
Then off to my left, the doe appeared
    slow moving, as if in a trance
No way I could pull the trigger, now
    altering my hunter's stance
Life gives us choices, too many to count,
    but today was one I won't regret
My companions in silence, I left there unharmed,
    never knowing that we ever met

Mr. Bass's Observations (The Tournament)

Have you ever wondered what bass all think about on tournament day
　When fifty boats with engines screaming all head a different way
Around some boats he watches how much junk food they consume
　Frito pie for breakfast! Give that man some room!
Old Mr. Bass gets weather reports all day loud and clear
　Then finds out what the Dallas Cowboys' chances are this year
There's even boats with cameras aimed, and movies being made
　And why is everybody in a rush to find a bit of shade
Women anglers are the ones to watch! They sneak in his domain
　They seldom talk, they're serious, even fish in pouring rain
He's heard the latest Aggie jokes, right above his head
　On tournament day it's worth the effort to leave the spawning bed
How many of them missed the chance to hang him on their wall
　Perhaps he'd make the cover of a bass magazine: Oh, the glory of it all

But it's more fun to break their lures, and yank rods through the air
   He's seen folks fuss, throw their hats, even pull their partner's hair
All year 'round, they sweat and freeze to endure this special day
   They won't even let a hailstorm or a twister in the way
He hangs around to watch the fun, when an outboard motor fails
   'Cause then they yell about some place that doesn't sound too swell
At two o'clock, old hawg heads in to watch them on the shore
   Weighing in his kinfolks, he can't visit anymore
He takes his eight-pound, four-ounce body close to where they're cooking
   Funny after they've searched all day, suddenly they stopped looking
He knows he'll never understand why certain days these folks act crazy
   Don't they understand large bass are usually full and lazy
Someday, though, he won't be so vain, he'll grab somebody's lure
   but only if it's on TV, on video for sure

Night Owls

A bullfrog sounding like a two-stroke engine,
   in the dancing light of the moon,
An old Coleman lantern enticing bugs,
   our night like a Hank Williams tune.
Red and white bobbers sank mysteriously,
   night wings creased the air.
A cottonmouth's head circled my line,
   I was caught in its ominous stare.
Night river fishin' in a flat-bottom boat,
   sitting close to the waterline,
Defies understanding and reasoning,
   an adventure hard to define.
Back at camp, it was Wolf Brand for breakfast,
   served over eggs and cheese,
Then a beeline for home as the sun came up,
   as night owls dozed in the trees.

Tinhorn Trip

My brother-in-law, old Eddie,
    called me up one autumn night,
"This weather sure is feelin' fine,
    think those bass will bite?"

"Sure they will, come on down,
    we'll give 'em our best shot."
Suddenly there was a quiet pause–
    was there something he forgot?

"I've got a brand new bank employee
    who never has been fishin'.
Do you think he could come along?
    We know what he's been missin'."

I told him yes, and to tell this guy
    that we'd be gone all day.
Something deep inside my soul
    suggested that I pray.

Early next morning, we stepped in
    my rig as the mist rose like a veil,
falling leaves began to drift,
    forming a river trail.

Eddie and I began to cast, and told
    Arthur to do the same.
With both jaws full of donuts,
    he remarked, "What if it rains?"

Finally, he took his brand new
    rod and reel out of its case,
Next thing I knew, I felt a lure
    bounce right off my face.

"Watch it, man! I need these eyes,
    throw out toward those trees."
Five more casts and brother-in-law
    was now upon his knees.

"Stop," I said, "and turn around
    and face the other way."
I knew this had the makings of a
    wild, rambunctious day.

We gently tried to tell this dude
    the way to catch a bass,
but he said he'd read most fishin'
    books and figured he could pass.

Close to noon, I got my food
  and sat back in the boat,
When suddenly a nine-inch,
  purple worm hit me in the throat.

"Arthur, while I'm eating, would you
  wait a while to throw?
We still have all the afternoon,
  and the bass are biting slow."

Next thing that good old Arthur did
  was hang a hornets' nest.
Finally, we found out for sure
  what he could do the best.

He paddled down that river
  with just his hands and arms,
delivering us from stinging foe
  attacking us in swarms.

Later 'neath a willow tree,
  he snagged the highest limb,
We had no bass in the livewell,
  I owed it all to him.

Then strangely Arthur threw
  straight out! and it fell beside a log.
Out of the water, his lip full of lure,
  rose a mighty hawg!

A ten-pound fury with blood in his eye,
  but Arthur brought him in.
So he ended our day with the only
  catch and a snooty kinda grin.

Back at the dock, as I loaded my boat,
  Arthur walked up to say,
"Sorry you didn't snag a bass,
  maybe another day."

I looked over at old Eddie
  with a snarl across my lip,
"Don't call me again for a year or two
  for another tinhorn trip."

Utopia

From kayak into breaking dawn,
shouldering streaks of gold
"Song of Hiawatha" rose
from deep within my soul
Utopia found, undisturbed,
God shared with me a gift
Solitude in abundance,
I felt my spirit lift
The eyes of Mother Earth,
this lake, cast a misty haze
Unpredictable, restless beauty,
underestimated ways
Drifting near a heron's stanch
as ducklings learn to fly
A swirling deep beneath me,
excitement passing by
When nocturnal instincts nudge me home,
sundown hurries up my pace
I gaze at God's Utopia,
for it's a healing place

Missing Paw Paw

His fifteen-horse Johnson put-putted along,
   a fisherman's music it played
Closing my eyes, I still hear it
   sometimes in evening shade

We shared rat cheese, bologna, and pickles,
   – poor man's caviar
Cool sody waters from a metal box,
   sweet tea from a mason jar

His youth and innocence left him
   on a place called Omaha Beach
Said that's why his hands shook nervously
   when things were out of reach

Where dragonflies dart in the sun,
   I slip his old vest on
So when I cast along the river,
   I never feel alone

Paw Paw loved his Lord and us children,
   and never changed his ways
Hope he senses how much we miss him
   on these lazy summer days

Thanksgiving Day Bass

November wrapped her charcoal sky
    around the honey hole,
With the threat of rain increasing now,
    the air was growing cold.
Home by ten I'd promised,
    for it was Thanksgiving Day,
But maybe around some old dead stump,
    I'd find a bass at play.

I tossed my jig about six feet,
    then I used a style called "bouncing,"
Hoping here on Turkey Day,
    an old hawg would come a pouncing!
Sure enough, blue water churned,
    I might be home for dinner,
If only I could land this bass,
    from the pull, he was a winner.

Over went my coffee cup,
    then the boat got turned around,
But I wouldn't let go of this bucketmouth,
    luckily I'd found.
Finally in my hands he lay,
    I had hooked myself a prize,
Eight-and-a-half pounds of largemouth fury,
    with fight still in his eyes!

Then suddenly a voice said, "Set 'im free,"
    from deep within my soul,
I decided right then to give this bass
    another chance at growing old.
"Well, not today old friend," I said,
    and released him over the side,
Then started home for the holiday,
    with an inner sense of pride.

Later on as my family dined,
    we prayed good times would last,
And I thought of the pleasure I'd had that morn,
    with my fine Thanksgiving bass.

SANDY CARROLL

Solitude

Sunlight cast diamonds across the lake
 I saw a dragonfly in a bass's wake
God said, "Seek and you will find."
 So, I left all my cares behind
To gaze at the world in a quieter place
 Enjoying our Heavenly Father's grace
Fall had cooled the morning air
 Then I saw whitetails everywhere
The shoreline showed signs of ancient man
 Then I found an arrowhead in the sand
Then pieces of pottery where a campfire had been
 I felt the Great Spirit suddenly descend
To remind me that time is a fleeting thing
 Enjoy what every day can bring

A Honey Hole Christmas

Morning dawned brisk, the lake crystal clear;
    The bass boat was filled with Christmas cheer.
Red and green spinners, blue and white jigs,
    Were strung up and down our whole fishin' rig.
My wife and I figured with our kids up and grown,
    We'd spend Christmas a fishin', instead of at home!
The turkey and dressing was under the seat,
    And a fresh mincemeat pie that couldn't be beat.
No more than an hour it seemed has passed by,
    When my wife hooked a hawg, then let out a cry.
The water was churning as I hummed Silent Night,
    This honey hole Christmas was turning out right!
We both topped our limit among the moss and the drifts,
    Then we ate Christmas dinner and opened our gifts.
A breathtaking sunset took shape in the sky;
    The kind that puts tears in a fisherman's eye.
We thanked God above for the beautiful sight,
    What a grand merry Christmas, what a wonderful night!

W.C. and the Sleeping Giant

The setting, it was perfect
  along the riverbank that morn
Old Mama Bass excited,
  baby bass were being born
The river like a mirror,
  reflecting willow trees
In the shallows, turtles playing
  among the fallen leaves
Circling round an old black stump
  with scars to mark his past
Was a trophy true, for a sportsman true
  who searched for largemouth bass
He'd bent the hook and spit the lures
  of many who had tried
And listened to them moan and groan
  when he had hurt their pride
But not far up the river,
  fate was setting up his gear
A veteran of lakes and streams,
  he sensed a fight was near

His eyes began to search the banks,
    he picked the spot to throw
The spinner hit the water
    where he wanted it to go
The man, the boy, combined that day,
    they were fighting all alone
Against the largest, smartest bass
    the river'd ever known
Bouncing off of rotten logs,
    twisting through the air
Snagging anything he could,
    being caught he couldn't bear
The man, the bass, the river
    for awhile became as one
Then it seemed they knew the instant
    the battle had been won
In the net, the bass lay trembling,
    tired but still defiant
The bass had met old W.C. and he had met
    The Sleeping Giant

Stillness

In faint cool envelopes of dusk, my heart began to soar

The stillness only broken by the dipping of my oar

Pods of minnows unaware of a bass's swirling fin

Rabbits rinsing off their scent near the river's bend

Indian summer beckoned me to camp with elk and loon

And sleep so peacefully by a fire beneath a climbing moon

I thank the Lord for places such as this to find retreat

A tiny glimpse of heaven beneath a sportsman's feet

69

Peace of Mind

Take me Lord where there's peace of mind,

And a bass will straighten my fishin' line,

Where friends are made and kept for life,

Camping far from stress and strife.

Then leave me there till the sun goes down,

And we're the only two around,

So I can spend some time with You,

Before dawn's early breath of dew.

The Wilderness Child

I sensed God's Spirit yesterday
In a sunset filled with cranes
Where all-encompassing quiet prevailed
Awaiting winter rains
Thick trees along the shoreline had not
Felt the logger's saw
Exhaling their breath upon me
I stood in mortal awe
Through all these years, God's covered my tracks
When I stumbled along life's trail
Wrapping me safe in His infinite arms
Ensuring that I would not fail
Now in the song of the winter wren
He bids me linger awhile
To remember that He is my utmost
And I am His wilderness child

For the Curious ~ Texas Country Talk

Aggies = anyone associated with Texas A&M University, whether students, alumni, faculty, fans, or neighbors. Aggies are known for their many school traditions and often find themselves the brunt of most good natured Texas jokes. Aggies were mostly farmers, so this name is short slang for Agriculture. An Aggie is the mascot of the college, whose colors are maroon and white, and was represented in earlier times as a military cadet. A&M's current mascot is a lovely Rough Collie, Reveille, or affectionately known as Miss Rev.

Bawling = crying & carrying on so

Blue Norther = coldest first day of winter. A type of weather, an Arctic cold front. A sudden drop of temperature with fast rise of barometric pressure, a phenomenon in Texas, resulting in shocking wind and often storms

Bluetick = best & loyal hunting dog - unless you've got something else.

Bomber's Rip Shad = lure to stir up the water. Bomber is a brand name that makes fishing lures. Rip Shad is a type of colorful, hard bait lure, with a shad profile, short and roundish

Bowl of Red = Texas chili, either Wolf Brand or homemade

Bushel = seen at farmer's markets and most homes in the country. Big round woven basket full of something. Sometimes refers to the basket itself, other times means the actual unit of measure for what's inside. (one bushel = 4 pecks)

Canebrake = a beautiful place outdoors. Vast areas of cane that densely grows around trees and underbrush. Countrified bamboo

Cathead Biscuits = biscuits big as a cat's head

Chiggers = nighttime nightmare. Teeny, tiny common summer pests, from a family of mites that bite

Clod-kicking Hayseed = what my daddy called me. A clod is a chunk of dirt, so a clod-kicker is someone who goes around kicking dirt clods for fun. Clod is also a derogatory slang term, sort of like Aggie, reserved for a person as smart as a ball of dirt. Hayseed is a slang term for a person not citified, someone from the country, simple & unsophisticated

Coleman = riverbank partner, usually refers to a brand name of lantern

Cottonmouth = a common venomous semi-aquatic snake, sometimes called 'water moccasin' & looks like it is walking on water when it swims. If you see a snake with its head held high out of the water with its whole body floating - don't mess around

Cottonwood = good place to sit. A common type of tree in Texas

Crappie = spring time surprise. A common type of fish found most anywhere. These are part of the papermouth gang & pretty great panfish if you can catch 'em

Dog Days = hot days in Texas, usually around July & August

Double-Barrel = double trouble shotgun

Evinrude = dang good motor

Fifteen-horse Johnson = arm breaking motor, good for cussing

Gaff = mean hook for big fish. A gaff hook is usually attached to a strong long pole and used to bring a fish into the boat that's too heavy for the strength of the rod & reel

Hawg = big bass fish

Hollers = the valley part between hills

Hydrilla = if you get caught up in this, just cut the line. A type of aquatic weed; an invasive plant that grows in ponds, lakes, rivers, and even ditches

Jon Boat = good place for snakes - they like hiding under the turned over boats. A jon boat is very versatile boat. They are mostly flat bottomed boats that make for a stable ride & easy to manuver and move around while fishing. Some are big & you can put a motor on, some are smaller and easy to move around on your own

Livewell = type of container to hold the fish caught, keeping them alive while you continue fishing

Lunker = big ol' fish

Mallard and Teal = beautiful birds - types of ducks

Navasota = history running name of a river that flows in Texas. Also the name of a city nearby (if you call a town with a population of less than 10,000 a city)

No-See-Ums = tiny, unidentifiable bugs. Chiggers fit in this category along with all the pests that get under your skin

Old Mossback = my dream fish. Nickname for famous bass

Papermouth = good for skillet. A type of fish & several kinds of fish go by this nickname. Like crappie and perch are called papermouths because if the fish takes the bait with a thought to escape, the hook can tear through the thin tissue of the lip, not get caught & live to see another day. Though there is a specific species named papermouth, they aren't found in Texas

Perch-jerkin' = slang for fishing. You can jerk the line to catch the perch

Rank = foul odor

Redfish = a day at the Gulf. Type of saltwater fish found in the coastal waters of the Gulf of Texas

Rig = could be talking about your boat, your truck & boat, or all your fishing gear for a certain type of fish

Roadrunner = fastest Texas bird - distinctly known for how fast it runs, traditionally admired for their strength, endurance, speed, and courage

Silver Shad = pretty by lantern light. Type of fish that attracts other fish. They sort of glitter & shine and flutter while they swim in groups

Tackle = the expensive part of fishing, because we're always losing them. *Wiggle Warts, Strike King 300, Rat-L-Traps, Nories, Crazy Shad, Jitterbugs, Mustad Hooks, Stanley jigs, spinnerbaits, spoons, plastic worms, surface plugs, Crazy Tails, Booyah Pranks, Nomad Chug Norris, Acme Little Cleo lures, Crankbaits, Thunder Cricket vibrating jig, Clod Hoppers - not to be confused with Clod Kickers - Big Bite Baits, Wally Divers, Lindy Little Nippers, and millions more*...these are all types of tackle. $$$

Tinhorn = an idiot. Someone that pretends to be important or have money, ability, or knowledge, but actually does not.

Top-water Plugs = a lure that floats to tempt a bass. When you pull the line, the lure moves back & forth along the top of water

Trotline = easy way to fish. A trotline is a heavy line of string mounted in a couple of places, sometimes between trees on either side of the river, or from the bank to a branch in the water, some even use two big floats from their boats. Spread out along the line, in intervals of your wishing, are suspending lines filled with bait & hook. Once you have the lines baited, go set up camp, grab a cool drink & shade and take a nap. Easy. Hopefully you'll have some fish for dinner when you wake up. Someone once told me that back in the day, people would tie the main line to two horses on either side of the water & have them trot for a bit to catch some fish. Hmm. Trotline.

Whippoorwill = a bird whose lonesome, soothing rhythmic call can be heard at night

White perch = summer afternoon, at ease in the shade with a cane pole. A type of fish

Wolf Brand = synonomous with ready cowboy chili in a can. Developed in 1895 in **Corsicana, Texas**, the original Wolf Brand Chili recipe sold for five cents a bowl. This oil boomtown also happens to be one of this poet's favorite stomping grounds